# 50 SPANISH PHRASES

Catherine Bruzzone and Susan Mart[...]

Illustrations by Leighton Noyes

Spanish adviser: Rosa María Martí[...]

## Contents

## Special note for learners!

The key Spanish phrases you will learn are numbered on each spread. There are also extra words you will need for the activities. By the end of the book you will know 50 SPANISH PHRASES and lots of useful Spanish words. There is a summary of all these at the back of the book.

## Pronouncing Spanish

The simple pronunciation guide will help but it cannot be completely accurate. Note that this guide is for a Latin American accent. Read the words as naturally as possible as if they were English. Put the stress on the letters in *italics*, e.g. adee-*oss*. Ask for help from a Spanish-speaking person and try to speak without the guide as soon as you can.

# ¡Hola!

Have some fun saying hello and goodbye in Spanish.
You need to match the right greeting to the pictures, according to the time of day illustrated. Say the correct phrase out loud. You can check your answers on page 32.

**1**

Hola, buenos días
*oh*-la *bweh*-nos *dee*-ass
Hello, good morning

**2**

Adiós
adee-*oss*
Goodbye

**3**

Buenas tardes
*bweh*-nass-*tar*-dess
Good evening

**4**

Buenas noches
*bweh*-nass *noch*-ess
Goodnight

## *Words to Know*

**¡Hola!**
*oh*-la
Hi!

**Hasta luego**
asta loo-*eh*-go
See you soon

**el día**
el *dee*-ah
day

**la tarde**
lah *tar*-deh
evening

**la noche**
lah *noch*-eh
night

3

# Me llamo...

Ask your friends or family to play this naming game with you. One person needs to be blindfolded and twirled round. They then have to 'find' someone and ask **¿Cómo te llamas?** The person answers **Me llamo...** and says **¿Y tú?** Take it in turns to be the 'finder'. You could all choose a Spanish name!

**5**

¿Cómo te llamas?
*kom*-oh teh *yam*-ass?
What's your name?

**6**

Me llamo...
meh *yam*-oh
My name is...

**7**

¿Y tú?
ee too
And you?

## Choose a Name!

**Juan**
hoo-an

**Carlos**
karloss

**José**
hoz-*eh*

**Francisco**
fran-*seess*-ko

**María**
ma*ree*-ah

**Pilar**
peel-*ar*

**Silvia**
sill-*vee-ah*

**Isabel**
eeza-*bell*

# ¿Cuántos años tienes?

You will need two dice for this game. One person throws them and the other asks **¿Cuántos años tienes?** The dice thrower answers **Tengo… años**, putting in the number the dice add up to. Take it in turns.

**8**

¿Cuántos años tienes?
koo-*wan*toss *an*yoss tee-*eh*-ness
How old are you?

**9**

Tengo nueve años
*tengo* noo-*weh*-beh *an*yoss
I am nine years old

**10**

¡Feliz cumpleaños!
*fel-ees* koompleh-*anyoss*
Happy birthday!

## Numbers! Numbers!

| | | | | | | |
|---|---|---|---|---|---|---|
| **1** | **uno** | *oo*no | **7** | **siete** | see-*eh*-teh |
| **2** | **dos** | dos | **8** | **ocho** | *o*cho |
| **3** | **tres** | tres | **9** | **nueve** | noo-*weh*-beh |
| **4** | **cuatro** | *kwat*-ro | **10** | **diez** | dee-ess |
| **5** | **cinco** | *sin*ko | **11** | **once** | *o*ns-seh |
| **6** | **seis** | sayss | **12** | **doce** | *dos*-seh |

Look at the numbers on the inside front cover if you want to ask some older people their ages!

# ¿Qué tal?

Cut out a circle of paper or card. Draw a smiley face on one side and a glum one on the other. Ask a friend **¿Qué tal?** as you show them one of the faces. They have to try and give the right answer depending on if it is smiley or glum. Swap round so that you can practise too.

# 13

No estoy bien
noh es*toy* bee-*en*
I'm not so well

## *Words to Know*

**Así así**
ass-*ee* ass-*ee*
So-so

**Bastante bien**
bas-*tan*-teh bee-*en*
Quite well

**Muy bien**
mwee bee-*en*
Very good

**Muy mal**
mwee mal
Awful

**Gracias**
*gras*-ee-ass
Thank you/thanks

9

# ¿Dónde está...?

Find all of the items in the **Words to Know** list and put them on a tray. Practise saying the Spanish words for them. Now close your eyes while a friend takes one item off the tray. (Cover up the Spanish words too.) You then have to ask **¿Dónde está el/la...?** whatever the missing thing is! Your friend will either say **Aquí está el/la...** or **¡Una vez más!** Take it in turns to have a go at remembering.

**14**

¿Dónde está...?
*dondeh estah*
Where is...?

**15**

Aquí está el/la...
*akee estah el/lah*
Here is the...

10

## 16

¡Una vez más!
*oo*na vess mass
**Try again!**

### A Note About El and La
There are two words for 'the' in Spanish – **el** and **la**.
Try to learn them when you learn a new noun.

## Words to Know

**el libro**
el *lee*bro
book

**el lápiz**
el *la*pees
pencil

**el lápiz de color**
el *la*pees deh ko*lor*
colour pencil

**el pegamento**
el pega-*men*-to
glue

**el papel**
el pa*pel*
paper

**la pluma**
lah *ploo*-ma
pen

**la goma**
lah *gom*-a
rubber

**la regla**
lah *ray*-gla
ruler

11

# ¿Qué es esto?

Look at this outdoor scene and practise saying the Spanish words. Then ask some friends or your family to play a drawing game with you. You each take it in turns to draw one of the named items and ask **¿Qué es esto?** Everyone else has to try and say what it is from the drawing (and without looking at the Spanish words). They say **Es un/una....**

**17**

¿Qué es esto?
keh ess ess-toh
What is it?

**una niña**
*oo*na *neen*-yah
girl

**una bicicleta**
*oo*na beesee-*klet*-a
bicycle

**un picnic**
oon *peek*-neek
picnic

12

**un pájaro**
oon *pah*-hah-ro
bird

**una pelota**
*oo*na pel-*ot*-ah
ball

**18**

Es un/una...
ess *oon*/*oo*na
It's a...

**una mochila**
*oo*na mo*chee*la
backpack

**un banco**
oon *ban*-ko
bench

**un niño**
oon *neen*-yo
boy

**A Note About Un and Una**
There are two words for 'a' in Spanish – **un** and **una**.
You say **Es un** for an **el** word and **Es una** for a
**la** word. For example, **Es una niña** or **Es un pájaro**.

# Aquí está la familia

Spot the family! Look at page 15. Which four people are members of the same family? Point them out and say **Aquí está el hijo** or **Aquí está la hija**. Use other words from **Words to Know** with **Aquí está** too. When you have found the whole family, you can say **Aquí está la familia**. Check your answers on page 32.

**19**

Aquí está el hijo
ak-*ee* ess-*tah* el *ee*-ho
Here's the son

**20**

Aquí está la hija
ak-*ee* ess-*tah* lah *ee*-ha
Here's the daughter

**21**

Aquí está la familia
ak-*ee* ess-*tah* lah fam-*ee*-yah
Here's the family

## Words to Know

**la madre/mamá**
lah *mah*-dreh/mam*a*
mother/mum

**el padre/papá**
el *pah*-dreh/pa*pa*
father/dad

**la hermana**
lah air-*mah*-na
sister

**el hermano**
el air-*mah*-no
brother

**el bebé**
el beh-*beh*
baby

**la abuela**
lah ab-*weh*-la
grandmother

**el abuelo**
el ab-*weh*-lo
grandfather

# Me gusta/me gustan...

Have a look at this picture and try and learn the Spanish words for everything. Then choose four things you like and four you don't like. Practise saying if you like them or not by using the phrases **Me gusta/me gustan...** and **No me gusta/no me gustan....** For example, **Me gusta el sol** and **Me gustan los árboles** or **No me gusta la lluvia** and **No me gustan los mosquitos**. Practise with a friend and take turns.

**las cabras**
lass *kab*-rass
goats

**los mosquitos**
loss moss-*keet*-oss
mosquitos

**23**

No me gusta/
no me gustan...
noh meh goo-stah/
no meh goo-stan
I don't like,...

**la lluvia**
lah *yoo*-bee-a
rain

**22**

Me gusta/
me gustan...
meh goo-stah/
meh goo-stan
I like,...

**los conejos**
loss kon-*ay*-hoss
rabbits

**las flores**
lass *flor*-ess
flowers

**los gatos**
loss gah-toss
cats

**el sol**
el sol
sun

**los árboles**
loss *ar*-bol-ess
trees

**los patos**
los *pah*-toss
ducks

**los cerdos**
loss *sair*-doss
pigs

**las arañas**
lass a*ran*-yass
spiders

**los perros**
loss *peh*-ross
dogs

**A Note About Me gusta/me gustan**
There are two ways of saying 'I like' in Spanish – **me gusta** and **me gustan**. You say **me gusta** when you like <u>one</u> thing and **me gustan** when you like more than one. For example, **Me gusta el sol** (I like the sun) or **Me gustan las flores** (I like flowers).

# ¿Dónde vives?

The children in the pictures are telling us where they live. Practise saying the phrases. Then cut out four pieces of paper to cover speech bubbles 25-8 and number them from 1 to 4. Ask a friend or adult to call out **uno**, **dos**, **tres** or **cuatro** and say **¿Dónde vives?** You have to try and remember how to say where you live according to the scene next to the number.

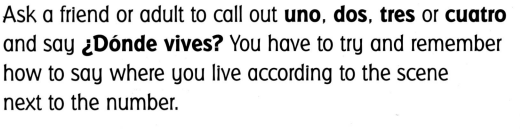

**24**

¿Dónde vives?
*don*-deh *vee*-vess
Where do you live?

**25**

Vivo en una casa
*vee*-vo en *oona kah*-za
I live in a house

**26**

Vivo en un departamento
*vee*-vo en oon deh-parta-*men*-toh
I live in an apartment

**27**

Vivo en la ciudad
*vee*-vo en lah see-oo-*dad*
I live in town

**28**

Vivo en el campo
*vee*-vo en el *kam*-po
I live in the country

# Quiero...

Have some fun with this Spanish shopping game for two or more people. Look at the shopping list and practise the words. The first player says **Quiero manzanas, por favor** and then points at the next thing on the list, the strawberries, on the market stall. The next player has to add them to the phrase, saying **Quiero manzanas y fresas, por favor**.
Each player adds another thing to the list and the winner is the first one to say the whole list correctly.
Then you can shout **Ya está, gracias.**

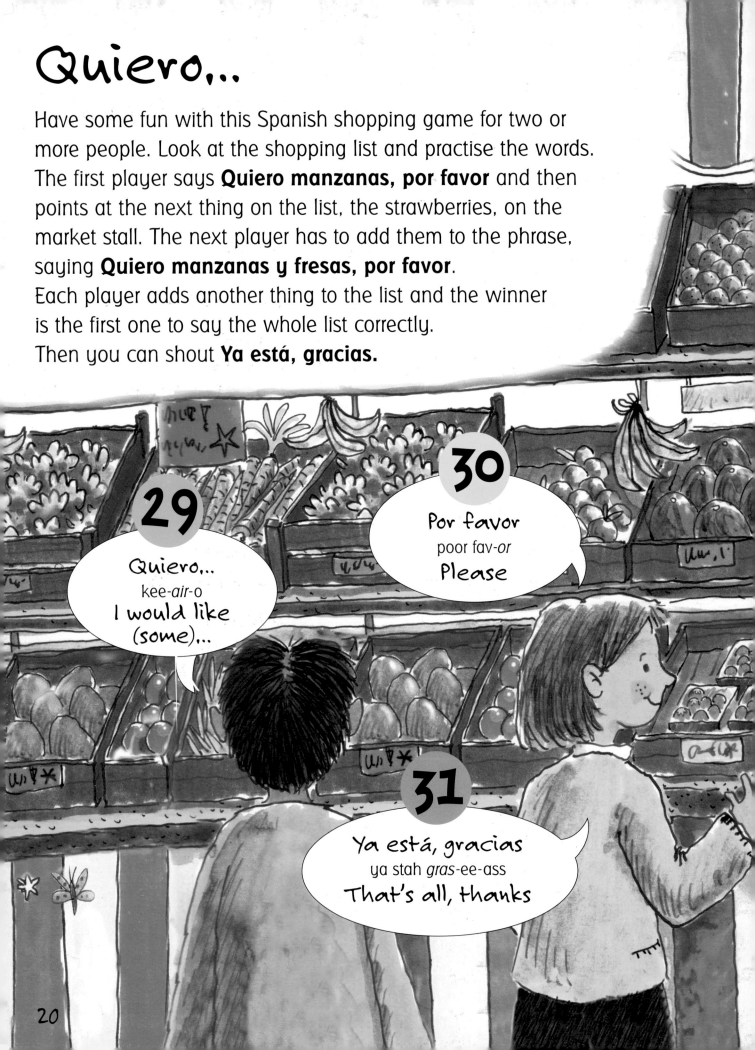

**29**

Quiero,...
kee-*air*-o
I would like
(some)...

**30**

Por favor
poor fav-*or*
Please

**31**

Ya está, gracias
ya stah *gras*-ee-ass
That's all, thanks

## The Shopping List

**manzanas**
man-*zah*-nass
(some) apples

**fresas**
*fray*-sass
(some) strawberries

**plátanos**
*plat*-anoss
(some) bananas

**uva**
*oo*-bah
(some) grapes

**zanahorias**
zanah-*or*-eeass
(some) carrots

**patatas**
pah-*tah*-tass
(some) potatoes

**tomates**
tom-*ah*-tess
(some) tomatoes

**ensalada**
ensah-*lah*-dah
(some) salad/lettuce

21

# Un vaso de agua, por favor

It's time to eat so have a go at asking for food and drink in Spanish. You can ask a friend or adult to say **¿Qué quieres?** All you need to do is choose something tasty from the menu and add **por favor**. You might also like to say **Tengo hambre** or **Tengo sed**.

**35**

Un vaso de agua,
por favor
oon *bah*-so deh *ag*-wah poor fav-*or*
A glass of water,
please

## Menu/El menú el men-*oo*

**un jugo de naranja**
oon *hoo*go deh nah-*ran*-ha
an orange juice

**un vaso de agua**
oon *bah*-so deh *ag*-wah
a glass of water

**un vaso de leche**
oon *bah*-so deh *leh*-cheh
a glass of milk

**un trozo de pastel**
oon *tro*-so deh pas-*tel*
a piece of cake

**un yogur**
oon yog-*oor*
a yogurt

**fruta**
*froo*-ta
fruit

**pan**
*pan*
bread

**jamón**
ham-*on*
ham

**queso**
*kay*-so
cheese

**patatas fritas**
pah-*ta*-tass *free*-tass
crisps

# ¿Qué quieres hacer?

You need two or more people to play this acting game. Read the phrases and then cover them up. One of you asks **¿Qué quieres hacer?** and acts out one of the activities. The other player, or players, answer **Quiero...** whatever they think the activity is. Take it in turns to be the actor.

**36**

¿Qué quieres hacer?
keh kee-*air*-ess *ah*-sair
What do you want to do?

**37**

Quiero mirar la tele
kee-*air*-o mee-*rar* lah *teh*-leh
I want to watch TV

**38**

Quiero jugar al fútbol
kee-*air*-o hoo*gar* al *foot*-bol
I want to play football

**39**

Quiero ir en bicicleta
kee-*air*-o eer en bee-see-*klet*-a
I want to cycle

**40**

Quiero nadar
kee-*air*-o nad-*ar*
I want to go swimming

## Words to Know

**¿Quieres…?**
kee-*air*-ess
Do you want to…?

**Sí, quiero**
see kee-*air*-o
Yes, I'd like to

**No, gracias**
noh *gras*-ee-ass
No thanks

# ¿De qué color es?

Here's a fun game to help you practise colours in Spanish with your friends or family. You will need a die and some counters. When you land on a square all the other players shout **¿De qué color es?** You say **Mi color preferido es el rojo** or whatever colour you have landed on. If you get the answer wrong you have to miss a turn. Good luck!

**41**

¿De qué color es?
deh keh kol-*or* ess
What colour is it?

START

FINISH

**42**

¿Cuál es tu color preferido?
kwal ess too kol-*or* preh-fair-*ee*-doh
What's your favourite colour?

Count in Spanish as you move your counter.

**43**

Mi color preferido es el...
mee kol-*or* preh-fair-*ee*-doh ess el...
My favourite colour is...

## Colours/Los colores los kol-*or*-ess

| | | | |
|---|---|---|---|
| **rojo** | **verde** | **negro** | **anaranjado** |
| *roh*-ho | *vair*-deh | *nay*-gro | anaran-*hah*-do |
| red | green | black | orange |
| **azul** | **amarillo** | **blanco** | **marrón** |
| ah-*sool* | amah-*ree*-yo | *blan*-ko | mah-*ron* |
| blue | yellow | white | brown |

# ¿Adónde vas?

These children are all dressed for their holidays. See if you can match the right phrases to the children. Say **¿Adónde vas?** and then choose the right answering phrase. Practise saying this out loud too. Check your answers on page 32.

**44**

¿Adónde vas?
*adond*-eh bas
Where are you going?

**45**

Voy a la playa
boy ah lah *plah*-ya
I'm going to the beach

**46**

Voy al campo
boy al *kam*-po
I'm going to the country

**47**

Voy a la montaña
boy ah lah mon-*tan*-ya
I'm going to the mountains

**48**

Voy a la ciudad
boy ah lah see-oo-*dad*
I'm going to town

## Words to Know

**de vacaciones**
deh vakassee-*on*-ess
on holiday

**¡Buen viaje!**
bwen vee-*ah*-hay
Have a good journey!

# Me pongo

It's time to get dressed – in Spanish! Have a look at the first picture and say **Me pongo pantalones pequeños.** Now look at the second picture and describe the difference in the trousers.
Say **Me pongo pantalones grandes.** Carry on describing the differences between the clothes on page 31. You'll need to use the **Words to Know** and have a look at the **Big or Small?** note too. You can check the answers on page 32.

**49**

Me pongo pantalones pequeños
meh *pon*-go panta-*loh*-ness pek-*en*-yoss
**I'm wearing small trousers**

**50**

Me pongo
pantalones grandes
meh *pon*-go panta-*loh*-ness *gran*-dess
**I'm wearing
big trousers**

**Big or Small?**

If the noun you are describing is an **el** (**un**) word, you use **pequeño**. If the noun is a **la** (**una**) word, you use **pequeña**. For example, **un abrigo pequeño** or **una falda pequeña**. **Grande** stays the same. If the words are plural (more than one) add an '**s**'. For example, **abrigos pequeños**, **faldas grandes**.

## *Words to Know*

**pantalones**
panta-*loh*-ness
trousers

**un abrigo**
oon ab-*ree*-go
a coat

**una camiseta**
*oo*na kamee-*say*-ta
a T-shirt

**una gorra**
*oo*na *gor*-a
a cap

**una falda**
*oo*na *fal*-da
a skirt

**un suéter**
oon *swet*-air
a sweater

**pequeño/
pequeña**
pek-*en*-yo/pek-*en*-ya
small

**grande**
*grand*-eh
big

# Las respuestas/Answers

Here are the answers to the activities on pages 2-3, 14-15, 28-9 and 30-1.

## pages 2-3

**4** Buenas noches

**2** Adiós

**1** Hola, buenos días

**3** Buenas tardes

## pages 28-9

**47** Voy a la montaña

**45** Voy a la playa

**48** Voy a la ciudad

**46** Voy al campo

## pages 14-15

Aquí está **la madre/mamá**

Aquí está el abuelo

Aquí está **la hija/hermana**

Aquí está el hijo/hermano

## pages 30-1

Me pongo un abrigo grande

Me pongo una camiseta grande

Me pongo una falda grande

Me pongo un suéter grande

Me pongo una gorra grande

Me pongo un abrigo pequeño

Me pongo una camiseta pequeña

Me pongo una falda pequeña

Me pongo un suéter pequeño

Me pongo una gorra pequeña

# 50 frases españolas/50 Spanish Phrases

**1** Hola, buenos días  Hello, good morning
**2** Adiós  Goodbye
**3** Buenas tardes  Good evening
**4** Buenas noches  Goodnight
**5** ¿Cómo te llamas?  What's your name?
**6** Me llamo…  My name is…
**7** ¿Y tú?  And you?
**8** ¿Cuántos años tienes?  How old are you?
**9** Tengo nueve años  I am nine years old
**10** ¡Feliz cumpleaños!  Happy birthday!
**11** ¿Qué tal?  How are you?
**12** Bien, gracias  I'm fine, thanks
**13** No estoy bien  I'm not so well
**14** ¿Dónde está...?  Where is…?
**15** Aquí está el/la…  Here is the…
**16** ¡Una vez más!  Try again!
**17** ¿Qué es esto?  What is it?
**18** Es un/una…  It's a…
**19** Aquí está el hijo  Here's the son
**20** Aquí está la hija  Here's the daughter
**21** Aquí está la familia  Here's the family
**22** Me gusta/me gustan…  I like…
**23** No me gusta/no me gustan…  I don't like…
**24** ¿Dónde vives?  Where do you live?
**25** Vivo en una casa  I live in a house
**26** Vivo en un departamento  I live in an apartment
**27** Vivo en la ciudad  I live in town
**28** Vivo en el campo  I live in the country
**29** Quiero…  I would like…
**30** Por favor  Please
**31** Ya está, gracias  That's all, thanks
**32** ¿Qué quieres?  What would you like?
**33** Tengo hambre  I'm hungry
**34** Tengo sed  I'm thirsty
**35** Un vaso de agua, por favor  A glass of water, please
**36** ¿Qué quieres hacer?  What do you want to do?
**37** Quiero mirar la tele  I want to watch TV
**38** Quiero jugar al fútbol  I want to play football
**39** Quiero ir en bicicleta  I want to cycle
**40** Quiero nadar  I want to go swimming
**41** ¿De qué color es?  What colour is it?
**42** ¿Cuál es tu color preferido?  What's your favourite colour?
**43** Mi color preferido es el...  My favourite colour is…
**44** ¿Adónde vas?  Where are you going?
**45** Voy a la playa  I'm going to the beach
**46** Voy al campo  I'm going to the country
**47** Voy a la montaña  I'm going to the mountains
**48** Voy a la ciudad  I'm going to town
**49** Me pongo pantalones pequeños  I'm wearing small trousers
**50** Me pongo pantalones grandes  I'm wearing big trousers